# BEHIND THE SCENES AT A NEWSCAST

## Whit Paddington

Cavendish Square
Square

New York

Published in 2015 by Cavendish Square Publishing, LLC
243 5th Avenue, Suite 136, New York, NY 10016

CPSIA Compliance Information: Batch #WS14CSQ

All websites were available and accurate when this book was sent to press.

Library of Congress Cataloging-in-Publication Data

Paddington, Whit.
Behind the scenes at a newscast / Whit Paddington.
pages cm. — (Vip tours)
Includes index.
ISBN 978-1-62713-031-8 (hardcover) ISBN 978-1-62713-033-2 (ebook)
1. Television broadcasting of news—Juvenile literature. I. Title.

PN4784.T4P33 2014
070.1'95—dc23

2014010513

Editorial Director: Dean Miller
Art Director: Jeffrey Talbot
Production Manager: Jennifer Ryder-Talbot
Production Editor: David McNamara

Packaged for Cavendish Square Publishing, LLC by BlueAppleWorks Inc.
Managing Editor: Melissa McClellan
Designer: Tibor Choleva
Photo Research: Joshua Avramson, Jane Reid
Copy Editor: Janice Dyer

The photographs in this book are used by permission and through the courtesy of: Cover by withGod/Shutterstock.com; p. 6 © Todd Shoemake/Shutterstock.com; p. 6 inset © michaeljung/ Shutterstock.com; p. 9 Sgt. 1st Class Kendall James/Oklahoma National Guard/Public Domain; p. 10 National Archives and Records Administration/Public Domain; p. 13 © Zhukovsky/Dreamstime.com; p. 13 background © Jerry Coli/Dreamstime.com; p. 14 © Rui Matos/Dreamstime. com; p. 14 inset © Constantin Opris/Dreamstime.com; p. 16 © Anthony Brown/Dreamstime. com; p. 19 © Viorel Dudau/Dreamstime.com; p. 20 © Darwin Lopez/Dreamstime.com; p. 22 © Ivicans/Dreamstime.com; p. 24 © Jannis Tobias Werner/Shutterstock.com; p. 24 inset © Tom Dowd/Dreamstime.com; p. 26 inset © Ahmet Ihsan Ariturk/Dreamstime.com p. 26–27 © Eddie Toro/Dreamstime.com; p. 29 inset SEWilco/Creative Commons; p. 29 © Daniel Raustadt/ Dreamstime.com; p. 30 Karin Hildebrand Lau/Shutterstock.com; p. 32 © NBC/Photofest; p. 34 © claudia veja /Shutterstock.com; p. 36 © Sophieso/Dreamstime.com; p. 39 Jeff Schultes/Shutterstock.com; p. 40 © Chris Schmidt/iStockphoto.com

Printed in the United States of America

# CONTENTS

# INTRODUCTION

You're working for a local news station. You and your team are reviewing the day's stories. You need to choose which ones to include in this evening's newscast. Suddenly, the **meteorologist** rushes into the room. He exclaims, "We are tracking a hurricane heading our way. It's a category 4 storm that should make landfall tomorrow morning."

A destructive hurricane approaching the coast is big news. It will become tonight's **lead** story.

Right away, the **news director** sends teams of reporters and camera crews to cover the storm. She sends the teams to different locations to cover the hurricane's arrival. Some will go to residential neighborhoods to see how people are staying safe. Others will go downtown to see how businesses are preparing. The reporters and camera crew pack first-aid kits and food supplies into their vans. They bring along portable electric generators in case the region's power supply goes down. The reporters wear appropriate clothing and rain gear to keep them dry in case of flash flooding.

The hurricane finally hits. Winds gust to 120 miles (193.1 kilometers) an hour. Tides surge 15 feet (4.6 meters) high. Over the next few hours, television viewers will depend on the news to track the storm's progress. The reporters must keep their audience informed. The station's weather specialist airs regular reports, describing up-to-the-minute weather conditions. He predicts which way the hurricane is headed. Reporters provide live updates from various locations, describing the conditions and showing how residents are coping.

A big news story can be dangerous, but it is also exciting. Keeping the viewers informed is a very important job. Let's explore what it's like to put together a television newscast. What happens behind the scenes? What are the different jobs?

Reporters will go to any length to inform the public about the latest developments.

# TELEVISION THEN AND NOW

On May 20, 2013, a massive tornado swept through Oklahoma City, leaving devastation in its tracks. The tornado destroyed homes, flung cars through the air, and demolished schools. Entire blocks of the city were flattened. TV stations sprang into action to get the latest updates to the citizens of Oklahoma. **News anchors** and reporters covered every angle of the story: Where was the tornado heading? What should people do to stay safe? How were the emergency responders coping with the devastation? Where should injured people go? Was there a possibility of new tornadoes forming?

The tornado story was a difficult one to cover. The storms were ongoing and new tornadoes could form at any time. Reporters needed to find a way to let people know what was happening, but they also had to stay safe. Some areas looked mostly untouched by the tornado, while others were devastated. Residents were in shock, so reporters had to be sensitive about what images to show the public.

It was critical that TV newsrooms continued to broadcast. While radio announcers might be able to describe the damage, TV newscasters could do much more. They could show photos of what the tornado had done to entire neighborhoods. They could also show how people survived the tornado. This frightening story, however, is just one fascinating event in the long, rich history of TV news broadcasting.

## INSIDER INFO

Journalism can be dangerous, especially for TV reporters who cover natural disasters or foreign wars. They must focus on the news story but not forget about their own safety. They must also cover the story without getting in the way. Some reporters and camera crews get special safety training. When covering war zones protective gear such as flak jackets may be needed as well.

As rescue workers dig out after a storm, news coverage keeps the community updated.

A family watches the evening news together. This was a daily tradition in many homes from the 1950s to the 1980s, when TV dominated the news media.

# The Beginnings of Television

The first TV programs in the United States were broadcast in 1930. On July 30 of that year, the National Broadcasting Company (NBC) opened a TV station. The Columbia Broadcasting System (CBS) started its first station the following year. In 1938, CBS's *World News Roundup* became the first major TV news show. Most people, however, still tuned in to radios for the day's news. Televisions were expensive and most households did not own one.

After World War II, television took off. Fascination for this new technology grew. Television could transmit information across thousands of miles in an instant. Unlike radio, television could broadcast words *and* pictures. TV stations beamed world events into homes everywhere. People could now see the news that made history. In 1963, horrified viewers watched footage of the shooting of President John F. Kennedy. Six years later, 90 percent of TV viewers in the United States witnessed a unique, live show. What a show it was! Audiences stared in disbelief as Apollo XI made its **lunar** landing. They shared astronaut Neil Armstrong's thrill as he took humankind's first steps on the moon.

## The First TV News Celebrities

Many early TV journalists got their start in radio. There, they sharpened their reporting skills by covering tough **assignments**. Many of these journalists went on to become stars on television. The first TV news celebrities were Edward R. Murrow and Walter Cronkite.

Murrow didn't think being a strong broadcaster took much. "All you have to do is love the news," he insisted. Murrow certainly proved he loved it. During his twenty-five-year career, he made more than 5,000 broadcasts! In 1962, Cronkite became the anchor on the CBS evening news program. Viewers came to rely on Cronkite's accurate reporting. They knew he would fully and fairly sum up the day's major events. He signed off each newscast with the phrase, "That's the way it was."

## MODERN NEWS CELEBRITIES

Today's news anchors are even bigger stars than Cronkite and Murrow were. The most popular can earn millions of dollars. Matt Lauer, co-host of NBC's Today, earns about $22–25 million a year. Diane Sawyer, the highest paid anchor on ABC News, earns $12 million a year. Millions of viewers tune in every day to watch these anchors deliver the news. They trust them to report both the tragedies and the triumphs.

Robin Roberts co-anchors ABC's morning show *Good Morning America*.
After earning a degree in communication, she started her career as
a sportscaster on local stations and ESPN.

TV's 24-hour news channels broadcast around the clock. When big news happens, they cover the story non-stop.

# Today's News 24-7

Important events can take place anywhere, and at any time. Many Americans want to see and hear these events the instant they happen. To meet this demand, Ted Turner founded the Cable News **Network** (CNN) on June 1, 1980. CNN reports news 24 hours a day. CNN news **correspondents** report from almost every country in the world. World leaders often tune in to CNN for late-breaking news.

Today there are many other 24-hour cable news stations available. Each station has its own style, programming, and news anchors. People have proven to have large appetites for many different forms of news. Some want to see the latest sports highlights. The cable network ESPN was created for them. Others want to watch the U.S. government in action on the Cable Satellite Public Affairs Network. You probably know this network simply as C-SPAN. Still others want to see the latest weather updates for their area and around the country. The Weather Channel provides this information.

# Internet News

Television news stations want to be a viewer's complete news source. To achieve this, many stations offer news stories and videos on their own websites. News stations update the information on their website on a 24-hour basis. This means that as soon as something new happens, it's on the web. People who want to be connected to the news all the time can access these sites on their tablet or smart phone.

Crew members get the anchor ready for a broadcast. Many people work behind the scenes of a news show.

# 2

# ALL ABOUT TEAMWORK

**P**utting together a newscast is a team effort. It can take up to two dozen people to put together each half-hour newscast! The team includes the director, the **producer**, news reporters and anchors, the editor, the camera crew, and makeup and wardrobe people.

Newscasts follow a strict schedule. As the day unfolds, the newscast schedule begins to fill up. Every second of a broadcast must be mapped out— including time for the station's theme song and commercials. A schedule lists the title of each story and that story's length. It also indicates when each story should appear in the broadcast, and which anchor will introduce it.

# News Directors

News directors control the entire newsroom. They supervise everyone, including reporters, anchors, writers, producers, and other technical staff. News directors plan the annual budget for producing the news, hire people, and purchase new equipment. They also review news items to make sure they are well written and well produced.

# News Producers

News producers direct each newscast. They manage the newscast from start to finish. At stations with newscasts at 5:00 P.M., 5:30 P.M., and 6:00 P.M., each show has a different producer. Producers plan the schedule and run the actual show. They must make sure their show starts and ends on time. Throughout the broadcast, they track how long each segment runs. If the show is running too long, a report can be dropped to gain needed seconds. Producers make sure the news stories are accurate and fair. They also make sure the newscast runs smoothly.

A news producer supervises every aspect of a broadcast to make sure it runs smoothly.

# Assignment Editors

Assignment editors choose the stories that will be covered by reporters. They may get phone calls, emails, or texts from members of the public who want to report a tip. They also listen to police and fire department scanners to pick up breaking news. The tip may also come from a **news release**. Companies or organizations send out news releases to announce an event, meeting, or **news conference**. Assignment editors often need to sort through piles of news releases to pick out the ones that the viewers will find interesting or important.

Working with a camera crew, a TV reporter condenses a lot of information into short news clips.

Once the assignment editors have chosen the stories they will follow, they send reporters and camera crews out to get the stories. If a story is really big, they may send out several reporters to cover the story from different angles. They keep track of the people and equipment that could be helpful in gathering each story's details.

# Reporters and Camera Crew

TV news reporters travel around the community to cover the stories that will be broadcast on the news. The station's staff of reporters covers the local and regional stories. They may also cover **beats**. Beats are areas of local interest in which a good reporter becomes an expert. Local beats include crime, education, and community service. Reporters use a beat system to find news and develop more in-depth news stories.

Reporters usually work with a camera crew, people who run the video camera and record the story. They all need to be available to rush to the scene of stories at any time of day or night.

## INSIDER INFO

National and international stories usually come from news services. These include the Associated Press (AP) and Reuters, which have reporters all over the world. Examples of national news that would interest local viewers might include a story about the latest presidential election.

Many news anchors start out as reporters before moving up to the top broadcast spot.

# News Anchors

The news anchors present the newscast to the audience. Before the newscast starts, they go through the rundown of the show. They practice announcing the stories and make sure they understand what they are saying. Makeup artists and wardrobe planners make sure the anchors look perfect for the broadcast.

The anchor opens the newscast and introduces stories. Many anchors also write and present their reports. For example, if an anchor is interested in health and medicine, he or she may write all stories related to these topics.

# The Lead Story

News producers decide which stories will begin, or lead, each show. Good news items can have local, regional, national, or international slants. The audience needs to relate to every story in some way.

Once leads are chosen, producers divide up the remaining stories. Each half-hour newscast needs eight to ten general news stories. They also require two weather pieces and about six sports reports. Some reports will run as short as 20 seconds. Others may run for as long as 6 minutes. Reporters, editors, and producers research and write these stories.

## INSIDER INFO

Some stations choose lead stories based on how thrilling the news is. These stations place importance on crimes and serious accidents. Such stations might lead with a story about a tiger escaping from a zoo. Meanwhile, another station might lead with a story about the local high school choir singing for the U.S. president.

A helicopter can get a news team on the scene quickly. Many TV stations have their own choppers.

# 3

# REPORTING THE STORY

## Breaking News

What happens when there is an unexpected event just before a newscast goes to air? Suppose a member of the local transit authority lets a friend at the newsroom know that a passenger train has crashed.

The assignment editor quickly pulls a reporter off a story about littering in public parks. After all, litter is an everyday problem. A train wreck is major news. Using the station's helicopter, the reporter and the camera crew fly to the accident site. They will broadcast via **remote feed** to the station. Now, time becomes a factor. How long will they take to reach the site? Will the story be ready to lead the newscast?

The reporter and the camera crew have a plan of action. At the train wreck, the reporter will question members of the police and fire departments. He'll locate bystanders who witnessed the wreck and interview them. His producer has told him that his report needs to fill 1 minute and 45 seconds, or 1:45, of the newscast.

Meanwhile, the camera crew will be busy shooting footage of the derailed train. They'll film the reporter telling the story and conducting interviews. A camera crew might shoot 20 or 30 minutes of film just to make a 1:45 piece.

Reporters interview people after disasters. They must learn to be sensitive to people's concerns.

When they return to the station, everyone will be in for more hard work. They will try to put together a report for the broadcast. Scenes from the video, called the **B-roll**, will be chosen. The reporter will add graphics—printed words or pictures—to the footage. The reporter may also develop a **tease**. A tease is a brief piece aired during the newscast or during commercial breaks. The tease urges viewers to watch the complete report. The report, graphics, footage, and tease make up a package.

All of this will take time—a luxury the station doesn't have. The news producer must decide which lead to run with. The train wreck is a huge story. The helicopter, however, hasn't landed at the scene yet. The producer decides to lead with the late-breaking story. The producer decides to open her newscast with live images of the wreck, taken from the hovering chopper. Later in the broadcast, once her remote crew lands, she'll cut to their live report.

# On Location

Newscasts often feature planned remote feeds from different locations. These locations can include sporting events, concerts, or awards shows. If the event is planned, the crew isn't as tense as the one covering a breaking news story such as the train wreck. Still, putting any story together is difficult work. The crew has to pack a full set of equipment when they leave for the location. They know they won't be able to return to the station for equipment such as batteries or electric cable.

There are two ways to send audio and video back to the TV station for broadcasting. One method is

Satellite and microwave trucks carry video production and editing equipment. This enables a news team to send back stories quickly.

Reporters conduct live interviews when they are covering a major event.

similar to cellphone technology. The other method uses signals from satellites. Reporters and technicians often use a special vehicle to send their stories from a remote location. The vehicle includes video monitors that show what is happening at various reporting locations. Technicians control the sound and what people see during the broadcast.

# Live or Taped

Newscast reports can either be live or taped. There's a big difference between the two. Taped reports are easily edited to fix any mistakes. Live reports can cause a lot of tension in the newsroom. Broadcasters and camera crews get only one chance to get a live report right.

So why go live? Live stories present the freshest news. Usually, live reports are favored when a story is still unfolding. It's one thing to tape a speech by the mayor for a later broadcast. That's a scheduled news event. When the mayor is finished talking, the story is over. On the other hand, what if police officers are involved in a high-speed car chase with a bank robber? If the news station waits to air an edited tape of this incident, the story may be old news by broadcast time. Audiences expect to see dramatic events, such as a police chase, the moment they occur.

## INSIDER INFO

Some stories combine taped and live segments. They're known as donuts. A donut, for example, might open with a live shot of the reporter. Later in the story, part of an interview taped earlier that day may be shown.

Connie Chung of CBS became the second woman to co-anchor a national newscast in 1993, after Barbara Walters of ABC in 1976. Katie Couric of CBS was the first woman to solo anchor in 2006.

# The Importance of Ratings

After the newscast, the news director anxiously studies the show's ratings. Ratings tell how many viewers watched the broadcast. The more viewers a show gets, the higher the ratings. The higher the ratings, the more the station can charge advertisers for commercial time.

More ad money creates better opportunities for the news team. The extra money might go toward hiring more reporters. It might allow the news director to buy better camera equipment or even a new helicopter.

Many people thought that the evening news would die off because of the Internet. Audiences for all TV newscasts have steadily declined since the mid-1980s. However, during the week of February 3, 2014, almost 29 million people watched the NBC, ABC, or CBS nightly newscast. This is the highest number since 2005. It seems that the nightly news might be experiencing a comeback!

## INSIDER INFO

About forty percent of all TV reporters and anchors are women. In the 1970s, women only made up thirteen percent of the television news workforce. Even today, most news directors are men. Only around twenty percent of people working in television newscasts are from a minority group.

Before working in TV, reporters and anchors study broadcast journalism in college.

# 4

# WORKING IN A NEWSROOM

**W**ould you like to work in a newsroom? Can you see yourself on camera as a reporter or anchor? What about being a member of the camera crew that captures the unforgettable images that make up major news events? Are you interested in one of the behind-the-scenes technical jobs for a newscast? Can you see yourself running the entire newscast?

## Becoming a News Anchor or Reporter

Many people dream of becoming TV announcers. Anchors seem to lead glamorous lives. Like everyone else in the newsroom, though, anchors put in long hours. Most local news anchors arrive at the station at around 2:00 P.M. for a 5:00 P.M. show. Before broadcasts, they must review the schedule, write

Reporters and their news crews may have long waits as a story develops. They may practically camp out at a site!

scripts, and polish their reading. Many anchors announce three broadcasts between 5:00 P.M. and 11:00 P.M. Often, they do not head home until midnight.

Reporters may work twelve-hour shifts to get the story, often in uncomfortable conditions. Reporters need to have a lot of stamina. They need to be flexible, knowing that they may not be home at a regular time. Reporters also need to be ready to travel at a moment's notice to follow the story.

News announcers and reporters must have strong presentation skills. They need to speak slowly and clearly. They practice **projecting** their voice to make sure it is easy to hear. They also practice pronouncing difficult words so they don't make a mistake on-air. Announcers must know their subjects. Viewers expect to trust TV anchors to learn the facts about the day's news.

A TV anchor is the "face" of both the news station and the town or city in which the station is located. They need to be comfortable talking to anyone about almost anything. To prove their commitment to the town, anchors often work on community-service projects. They may also attend major public events and help local charities. These efforts help anchors develop a bond of trust and loyalty with their viewers.

Many anchors and reporters have **blogs** that take the audience behind the scenes of the most interesting news stories. Updating stories on Twitter, Facebook, and other social media has also become part of the job.

## INSIDER INFO

Both anchors and reporters need a wide range of skills. They need to be confident and outgoing. They need to be able to improvise, because you never know what can happen on live TV. They need to work as a team and stay calm under pressure. And they need to meet strict deadlines.

# Becoming a Sports or Weather Anchor

Sports and weather anchors normally report later in a newscast. During special occasions they may see their roles expanded. Suppose the local college basketball team has made it into the Final Four NCAA Basketball Championship. In this case, the sportscaster would probably lead off the broadcast.

A local sportscaster's job may be very different from a sportscaster who broadcasts on a network. An ESPN anchor may specialize in one sport. A local sportscaster must report on all sports, national and regional. They must be able to cover the high school volleyball squad as well as the major league baseball action.

Forecasting the weather has become a high-tech job. Radar, computer models, and long-term forecasts have replaced gazing at the clouds. National weather services provide everything from satellite pictures of storms to local wind conditions. News stations expect weather anchors to have degrees in meteorology. Weather anchors are also expected to understand all aspects of local weather. For instance, a meteorologist in Nebraska would need to understand how a long drought could damage farm crops.

Sports reporters interview athletes right after they have won a big event. The sports news team shares in the excitement.

Practice doing interviews if you are interested in broadcasting.

# How Can You Get Involved?

If you want a career in TV journalism, you can start following your dream right away. To begin, watch the news, read the news, and follow news stories online. The more you learn about current events, the better prepared you will be to report them. Some news websites allow you to submit ideas for stories, or even videos of you reporting on local stories. Also consider making news reports for your school's newspaper.

Television journalism is a demanding profession, with long hours and lots of hard work. However, the rewards can be amazing. Working on newscasts can bring excitement, adventure, and opportunities to meet amazing people. If you are willing to put in the effort, being part of a newscast could be a unique and rewarding career for you.

## HERE ARE SOME TIPS TO GET YOU STARTED

Write news articles about current sports and events. Make sure you've reported on the who, what, when, where, why, and how of each event.

- Report on important school policy changes, such as dress code or detention.
- Use simple, clear language and short sentences.
- Practice reading in front of a camera. Speak directly to the camera as if it were a friend. It's important to keep eye contact with your viewers.

Whether they work for newspapers or TV stations, reporters need to develop strong writing and inter-viewing skills. They must do their own research and find the right facts. Here are some tips for a successful interview:

- Learn about your person and topic ahead of time.
- Make a list of thoughtful questions to ask.
- Avoid questions that get "yes" or "no" answers.
- Create a relaxing atmosphere.

# NEW WORDS

**assignment:** the story that a reporter researches and reports about

**B-roll:** the video portion of a report

**beat:** a general area of interest assigned to a reporter

**blog:** a personal website that includes opinions and information recorded on a regualr basis

**correspondent:** someone who reports for television, radio, or newspapers about a special subject or place

**lead:** the first story of each newscast

**lunar:** to do with the moon

**meteorologist:** a scientist who studies Earth's atmosphere, climate, and weather

**network:** a group of television stations that are connected to each other

**news anchor:** the main person who reports the news on a TV news show

**news conference:** a meeting organized to share information with the media and answer questions

**news director:** the manager of a news team

**news release:** a statement provided to the media to announce an event or information

**producer:** the person who plans and runs a news program

**projecting:** making your voice heard from a distance

**remote feed:** the connection between a remote location and the TV station

**tease:** a small section of a news report meant to hook viewers into watching the entire broadcast

# FURTHER INFORMATION

## Books

Diconsiglio, John. *The News Never Stops*.
Hampshire, UK: Raintree, 2010

Reeves, Diane Lindsey. *TV Journalist*.
New York, NY: Checkmark Books, 2008.

Teitelbaum, Michael. *Television*.
North Monkato, MN: Cherry Lake
Publishing, 2013.

Teitelbaum, Michael. *Sports Broadcasting*.
North Monkato, MN: Cherry Lake
Publishing, 2008.

# Organizations

**American Sportscasters Association**
225 Broadway, Suite 2030
New York, NY 10007
(212) 227-8080
www.americansportscastersonline.com

**Radio Television Digital News Association**
529 14th Street, NW, Suite 1240
Washington, DC 20045
(202) 495-8730
www.rtdna.org

# Websites

**Alliance for Women in Media**
www.allwomeninmedia.org
Promotes the entry, development, and
advancement of women in the media.

**Behind the News—ABC**
www.abc.net.au/btn
This site provides a behind the scenes look
at the world of news.

# INDEX

# ABOUT THE AUTHOR

**Whit Paddington** is a high school journalism teacher with a degree in broadcast journalism. Whit has also worked on many plays as a director and producer with his local theater company. A native of Massachusetts, he lives in the country with his fiancée.